PIONEER DAYS AT TEKOA

BERTHA ENGELLAND WILLIAMS
Born August 1888 — Died July 1981

PIONEER DAYS AT TEKOA

By

BERTHA ENGELLAND WILLIAMS

YE GALLEON PRESS
FAIRFIELD, WASHINGTON

INTRODUCTION

These reminiscenses were told to Gladys E. Guilbert in Mrs. Williams' home in Lacy, Washington. Several interviews were taped for inclusion in oral history files of Spokane and Olympia public libraries. This booklet is actually a reprint of a series of articles prepared by David C. Guilbert from those interviews. The articles were printed in the *Spokane Daily Chronicle* during the months of June and July 1975 under the title "Those Olden Times." The articles were illustrated with various photographs of Mrs. Bertha Engelland Williams and her family, most of which are duplicated here in this Ye Galleon Press booklet.

Mrs. Williams' father, George Engelland homesteaded near the present-day town of Tekoa, located in southern Spokane County, Washington. Returning home to Hamdorf, Germany to attend his mother's funeral, he was asked to guide a small group from that town back to America. The group included two of the Stender sisters, Lisa and Frauke. After their arrival in the Palouse, George and Frauke were married. They settled on George's homestead, where they raised their family.

Bertha Engelland Williams' stories provide insight into early Palouse history, and glimpses of pioneer homestead life. Photographs of Mrs. Williams' family were provided by the Tekoa, Washington Museum, to which we give our thanks.

Dale La Tendresse
April 1986

Bertha Williams

ISBN 0-87770-383-3

HOMESTEAD DAYS RECALLED

Often as a girl, I wondered what dreams must have danced through the heads of the young Stender sisters; Frauke, who became my mother, and Lisa, which led them to leave home. Enticing visions they must have been, for these girls joined four German emigrants from Hamdorf, Germany, for the long, uncomfortable journey to America and the pioneer hardships of the Pacific Northwest.

Leading this little band to eastern Washington was young George Engelland, my father, who had but recently taken up a homestead near what is now Tekoa. He had returned to Hamdorf to attend the funeral of his mother. While there he was persuaded to act as guide and interpreter for the group.

As steerage passengers, these young people sailed from Bremen in June, 1886. Steerage was the migrants' way to get here in those days as it was the cheapest form of transportation.

Most of those who left European shores then did not possess a surplus of money. They came to the U.S. with hopes of bettering their economic status, as well as enjoying more freedom and leaving behind the severe class distinctions that existed in Germany and other countries.

After three or four weeks at sea, George Engelland's band landed in Baltimore. There an immigrant train for the west was waiting on the dock.

Mother often spoke of the weariness of that long trip by ship and slow moving train. Along the way, her curiosity was aroused by the "white buttons" as she called them, on the doors of the houses in the small towns they passed through. She discovered they were used to open the doors. In Germany only latches, called "klinks," did this job. So one of her first impressions of America was that of a land of round, white door knobs.

On reaching Cheney, it was necessary for all the group to spend the night in a rooming house there. The Stender sisters were both severely bitten by bed bugs so aside from being weary from the long train ride and the weather being sultry and warm, it was also a very itchy, lumber wagon trip from Cheney to North Pine, where another of the Stender sisters lived.

During the many days of tiresome travel, George Engelland evidently came to the conclusion that his homestead cabin was going to seem very lonely away from the companionship of the attractive girls in the immigrant band.

George and Frauke Engelland with daughter Bertha and son Herman

Along the way he had proposed and, on July 7, 1886, Frauke Stender and George Engelland were married by a judge at the Watson school house in the neighborhood of North Pine, the post office for all that country.

Before coming to America, my father had gone to sea as a cabin boy in sailing ships and done a year's hitch in the German navy. As part of his training, he went to a navigation school where, among other subjects, he studied English. Thus he had a working knowledge of the language when he came to this country. Still it was a drastic move from a career on the high seas to becoming a dry-land farmer.

He arrived in the U.S. in 1883 and, after a stop in Illinois, came by rail to San Francisco, by boat to Portland and by rail to Cheney.

He had friends near Spangle and, after working in the harvest, spent the winter there. Most of the land in the Palouse had already been homesteaded before 1880 so my father had considerable difficulty finding a quarter section for a homestead.

In those early days it was thought that no area could amount to much unless there were deciduous trees growing on it someplace. In order to encourage tree planting the government permitted a homesteader to double his land holdings to two quarter sections, 320 acres, if he planted ten acres to trees. These usually consisted of Lombardy poplars or box elders and were known as timber cultures.

Many a homesteader who filed on a timber culture later found that he could not raise money to buy the trees so he had to relinquish one quarter section.

One Palouse homesteder, Albert Mesterman, found himself in this predicament. When father heard of it, he walked from Spangle to the Mesterman farm, almost to what is now Tekoa. He was able to work out a deal and both men rode by horseback to Colfax to file the transfer.

Father moved onto the 160 acre homestead in an April snowstorm in 1884. He often told me of his impressions of the beauty of the open prairies. While bunch grass predominated, wild roses, service berry (saskatoon) shrubs and so-called sun flowers grew with here and there a pine tree. Through the seasons carpets of buttercups, pink phlox, grass widows, yellow bells and pasque flowers bloomed. There were the blues of lupine, wild hyacinth, camas and larkspur. Later came wild geraniums.

The Jurgen Mumm Family. This picture was taken in Germany. Mrs. Mumm was my aunt, George Engelland's only sister. Henry Mumm, their son, came to America. They are not related to any other Mumm's who lived in the Palouse country, however.

In the low places, huge beds of wild iris flourished. Flowers now extinct in that area, were beds of tiny, pale blue violets, lavender mariposa lilies, and, on damp shrubby north hillsides, were dainty, pale purple wild orchids, known as lady slippers.

This, then, was the place father brought mother after they were married at North Pine.

DESOLATION OF PRAIRIE LIFE FEARFUL

While courting on the long journey across the Atlantic and this country, my father apparently painted his homestead in glowing terms in persuading mother to marry him.

After their marriage en route home, they were driven by wagon from North Pine to the farm. This was July 8, 1886.

Mother said she could scarcely believe the little clapboard, two-room shack and small barn standing forlornly on the unbroken prairie was actually her future home. The contrast with the manicured, tree-shaded farmlands and their substantial old houses and outbuildings of her native homeland was almost too much to take in.

Furnishings consisted of a rude table and bench, a small cast iron stove, a bed of some sort, a cast iron kettle and the meagerest of other kitchen equipment such as a bachelor might get by with. Later in the year, the winter snows sifted through the cracks in the cabin and had to be swept off the stove before a fire could be started.

Wood for fuel was secured by going to the Cove area to the north, sawing down a pine tree and hauling it home in sections. In the early days, every farm house had a log in the yard from which fire wood was sawed or chopped as needed. Father often told of regular brigades going on sleds in the winter to bring out the required wood. It was easy to load a log on a sled and skid it home.

Fortunately mother had brought stout homespun clothes and a feather bed or two from Germany so that, despite the drafty cabin, they did not suffer excessively from the cold.

She feared the Indians, the coyotes, the treelessness (at that time she would not even admit that pines were trees), the horses and cattle roaming the wide open, unfenced country—in fact, everything about the new life was terrifying to her and it took some time for her to adjust to these strange conditions.

Complicating her life, she knew no English. But fortunately her nearest neighbors, two families of Mestermans, were both German so she could talk with them. However, this further delayed her learning the language of her new home.

One of the decorations in the new shack was a board on which father had printed "I DO NOT SPEAK ENGLISH." When a stranger came to the door when mother was home alone, she would point to the sign.

Soon she was asked to help with the meals for the crew at harvest time on the S.L. Jamison's place. The chief cook, Mary Blue, knew no German, so they communicated more or less in sign language and, here, mother learned her first English words.

Later, when she had acquired a little more English, mother helped Mrs. John Schau cook for the harvesters. Mrs. Schau was a rapid talker and mother was unable to understand all she said. Every once in a while, Mrs. Schau would say, "Don't you think so, Frauke?" Mother would invariably say, "Yes." Once when mother said "Yes," Mrs. Schau laughed and replied, "This time, you should have said, 'No'."

Prairie chickens, now extinct in that area, were very numerous then. Father told of taking his shotgun down to Hangman creek and returning with a gunny sack full of birds. These were dressed out and salted down to become an important source of meat. They also butchered a pig or two and made sausage and other pork products which they smoked and which were therefore edible the year 'round. They seldom killed a beef as it was impossible to keep beef from spoiling unless it was brined, and even then it did not keep well for any length of time.

Dried prunes and dried apples were the chief fruits eaten. These were bought at Farmington or Connell's. Potatoes and other vegetables were grown on the homestead and some chickens and a cow were added so the family had fresh eggs, milk and butter. Mother said that even in those first years they never suffered from lack of food.

It took five years to prove up on a homestead and then a deed was given by the United States government. All this time there was no Tekoa so all trading was done at Farmington or Colfax which were on a wagon freight route connecting with the boats running up the Snake river. Some earliest homesteaders made annual trips to Walla Walla for trading purposes.

In the latter 1870's Frank Connell, the first homesteader in the area, opened a trading post on his farm nearby where some staples could be bought and where he dealt with the Indians. Ed Connell, his son, related that the Indians had never seen rice and when he showed some to the Indian women, they giggled and called it "ant eggs."

The nearest post office was at Lone Pine, which was so named because of a huge pine which stood alone on the prairie until about 1955 when it blew down. The post office was located in the kitchen of the house where the stages stopped on their runs from either Lewiston or Almota on the Snake river to Cheney. It seemed to me I heard that Lone Pine was abandoned when Tekoa was established as a post office.

SEA OF GRASS TRANSFORMED

It's hard to realize now that when my father brought his bride to his homestead in 1886, less than 100 years ago, there were more people living on farms in the Palouse country than there are now and that most of the towns were stage or freight stations with hardly any population at all. Because there were very few elderly people in the area then, we were intrigued by them. I remember two wrinkled and weatherbeaten old ladies who smoked pipes as they sat and reminisced in the sun.

In my lifetime, the Palouse changed from the vast sea of grass with unbroken sod and families on each 160 acres to intensive families with but one or two families on large acreages. It has gone from horse-powered threshing outfits to self-propelled combines and Tekoa became a roaring, wide-open town and then subsided into today's pretty, tree-shaded, quiet rural community, when it no longer was a railroad division point.

In 1888 or 1889 when the Oregon-Washington Railroad and Navigation Company built its settlement was founded around a sawmill and this became Tekoa.

At the outset, there were no trees and the whole effect was somewhat as if cardboard buildings had been tossed down on the rolling prairie. Neither were there lawns, flower gardens or well-kept yards. A few residents had vegetable gardens.

Henry Mumm
My first cousin. He was the son of Jurgen Mumm and my father's only sister. He came to the United States and had two children, Hans Jr. and Anna.

Streets were deep in dust in summer, deep in mud in the wet seasons. I have seen horses wading in soupy, railroad through this area, a churned up mud up to their knees. And when frozen, the streets were bone-jarring messes.

Sometimes on a busy day, all hitching racks along the streets were in use by teams and riding horses. A farmer coming to town always knew who was there ahead of him for he easily recognized each team tethered to the racks.

The first business houses were located on the street facing the railroad. It was a row of false-fronted buildings with second-story porches that extended over the sidewalks. The sidewalks were wooden and had crosswalks across the street at intervals. These were made of planks laid lengthwise with the outside ones placed at an angle to allow wagons to cross them without too much of a bump. In muddy periods, we walked with care as these crosswalks were slippery and slimy with mud. Women clutched their then stylish, very long, floor length skirts to raise them out of the wet.

Most of my memories of Tekoa come from the time I started school there in 1894. One of these was that there was a flag pole in the intersection in front of the drug store. A weather flag was hoisted there every day. White meant good weather, blue rain or storms. Steve Coffin, the druggist, received daily reports by telegraph and changed the flags.

Later the flag pole was replaced by a bandstand and on Saturday evenings the town band played a concert. It seems to me there was still a concert there as late as 1914 or 1915.

Otis Hill had a drygoods store and above it was the Tekoa Opera House, with its stage, scenery and curtain. To the Opera House came stage plays, vaudeville shows, hypnotists, lecturers and whatever else was available in the way of entertainment and culture.

Sometimes when these performances came along, if the show did not please the audience, eggs were hurled at the actors. I recall one rowdy saying, "That show cost me 40 cents—25 to get in and 15 for eggs."

Graduation exercises were held there each year for both the public school and St. Joseph's Academy, a Roman Catholic school where many of the children from the hell-roaring mining towns of the Coeur d'Alenes were sent to get them away from the wide open communities.

Hans Mumm Jr.
Son of Henry Mumm

Anna Mumm Suksdorf
Daughter of Henry Mumm

We entered the Opera House up a wooden stairway at the rear of the building. The place was heated by a huge iron, pot-bellied stove located at the rear of the room. There were no fire escapes and often the space was jammed with families. I shudder to think what might have happened had a fire occurred.

But we didn't worry about that then. Many dances were held in this hall. Music was furnished by Minnie Schott on the piano; Henry Warner, guitar; and Dave Campbell with his violin. "Irish Washerwoman" and "Turkey-in-the-Straw" were two of the popular tunes to which we danced.

At least one masquerade ball was held each year and for this the opera house was crowded. All who danced brought their children along. I could not have been more than ten when I danced in quadrille sets, now called square dancing. Waltzes came in later and, after we learned to waltz, scorned quadrilles as being "old fashioned."

But as time went on, the Coeur d'Alene mining boom had quite an impact on Tekoa as much of the materials used in those communities were sent into the mines by rail coming through our town. At one time, passengers from the Coeur d'Alenes going to Spokane had to stop over in Tekoa for the night and catch the morning train. Tekoa was growing up and reckless.

WILD DAYS OF TEKOA RECALLED

Looking at the quiet, pleasant, tree-lined streets of Tekoa today, who would ever believe that this community had a reputation as being wild and woolly not too many years ago?

Yet until approximately 1920, as I remember it, Tekoa had a somewhat wild and reckless element as well as its share of solid citizens. Murders, stabbings and fights were not uncommon.

There were a lot of transients, hoboes riding the rails and such. Most, however, were men who drifted in to work the wheat harvest.

They sat with their bedrolls in rows on the sidewalk which was higher than the street so they could dangle their legs as they faced the traffic. Farmers who needed help strolled up the street and picked from these men. The farmer looked at the size and quality of the man's bedroll and his general appearance and made his selection.

Those men who asked too many questions about location, accommodations or pay were rejected. Often a "hired man" only lasted one day because he was lazy, balky, lacked knowledge of farming or had too much of a hangover.

No hired man was asked his name. They were identified in the payroll records by names such as Blacky, Yakima, Red, Nova Scotia or Ole. In one ledger my father listed "Hobo."

At night these transients camped in the "jungle" which was down the creek from where the roundhouse stood. In the evenings, there were as many as a dozen campfires.

In the early 1900's it was not unusual, especially during the harvests, to see drunken men lying in vacant lots. It was whispered about among us awe-struck youngsters that many were "drugged and rolled" (robbed) and then tossed out of the saloons.

Just as you see in the Western movies today, our saloons had double, swinging doors and a "ladies" bar in the back to which, now and then, I saw some women dodge furtively.

One "lady" who clerked in a dry goods store used to dash across the street to the ladies' bar several times a day. By late afternoon, she was unable to read the price on her merchandise clearly and either over or under charged her customers.

Each saloon had at least one professional gambler connected with it. Some were called "honest" gamblers and others "crooked." I often wonder how the distinctions were made. These gamblers wore fine clothes and fancy, flowered vests and were known by names such as "Frenchy," "J.P.," and were identified as "he gambles at so and so's saloon."

Gambling was not entirely confined to the saloons. I recall some 65 years ago, a circus moved into the center of Tekoa. The big news about it was that a very tightfisted farmer lost $60 in a shell game.

And talking about liquid refreshments, almost every other household in town owned a cow. Those who did not bought milk from their neighbors or from a milk man who had a small dairy and made deliveries daily. The dairyman came to the door with a ten quart or, perhaps, three gallon can. He carried it by its curved handle. In the other hand he had a quart measure. When the housewife came to the door with a pitcher or kettle, he measured the milk from his big can and poured it into the home

Grandmother Stender with her grandchildren
From left, Bertha Engelland Williams, Edwin Carbery and Herman Engelland

container — a far cry from our present, cartoned, pasteurized variety.

The town cow herd was fed hay in the winter and, in the summer, was collected by a herdsman, usually a teenage boy with a horse, and driven out to pasture for the day for one dollar per head per month. He stayed with the herd all day and returned each cow to its owner at milking time in the evening. Sometimes the herd numbered as many as 60 cows.

But Tekoa did not have a mortuary until 1909. Before that a corpse was usually prepared for burial by neighbors or a member of the family. After the corpse was placed in the coffin, it was set on saw horses or several chairs in the living-room and neighbors then sat up with the dead all night. Often the funeral services were held in the house, especially among the farm people. The hardware store sold the coffins.

Later, at Oakesdale, someone acquired a horse drawn hearse. When a death occurred at Tekoa, that hearse would drive by the west side of our farm on the Tekoa road. Whenever the hearse went by, we wondered who had died in Tekoa.

Before cemeteries were established in our communities, burials were made on the prairie at the homestead and fences erected around these plots.

Many are the changes that have taken place in the last 80 years!

MEMORY OF EARLY DAY EDUCATION FRIGHTENING TO RECALL

What we went through at school in Tekoa in 1895 is a far cry from present day "progressive education." More recent generations may find it hard to believe what school was like in these early days.

My memories of my first teacher are anything but pleasant as she was somewhat sadistic and broke several pointers and yard sticks across the backs and heads of unlucky pupils every day. This frightened me into a state of virtual paralysis, specially as I could not understand why she was attacking these youngsters. My father and mother spoke German in our home so when I started grade school I did not speak any English and the teacher gave me absolutely no help and no attention. I remember having to stay in at recess because I had not learned to write my name. I wished bitterly that my name — Bertha Engelland — did not have so many curlicue letters in it.

I do remember with affection my teacher, the Missees Bushnel and Sheer, for they were always ready to help me with problems and made me feel that I was a member of the class instead of a queer little "Dutch" country girl to be regarded as a curiosity.

Another teacher I had was a typical "Gibson girl" type, a very handsome, dark-haired young lady. I can still see her high pompadour, her cerise-colored, leg-o-mutton sleeved blouse—we called them shirt waists then—and light gray flannel skirt that swept the floor. It was trimmed with black braid and made to dip in the front at the waist.

Until I was a seventh grader, a slate was part of my school equipment. I started with a single slate and then Santa Claus, via an uncle, delivered a double slate to me.

A double slate consisted of two slates hinged together so that it opened like a book. They had wooden frames and red felt was sewed through drilled holes around the outer edges of the frames.

What was written on the slates with a special slate pencil could be easily erased with a damp cloth or water. Neither was usually convenient, more often than not we'd stick a finger in our mouth to wet it and use it to wipe the slate. Cruder ones simply spit on the slate and brushed it off with a shirt sleeve.

Slate pencils sometimes had bits of sand in them and, when the slate was gouged with it, gave out a horrible squeaky sound that set teeth on edge all over the room. This was a pet form of teacher torture, to run the screeching pencil up and down the slate while innocently writing.

Most of us who lived in the country walked to school. Our family lived only a little more than a mile from the school but getting there in bad weather was a problem. When we were small, my father took us in a hack, a two-seated light wagon. When we were a little older we rode horses in bad weather or went in a two-wheeled vehicle we called a cart. It was drawn by one horse.

Another school person I remember was our first janitor. He was tall, straight and slender and wore a long white beard. I think he was the kindest person I have ever known for he was forever helping all the children. In those days there were no pencil sharpeners and this man spent all of the recess period and most of his noon hour sharpening pencils with his pocket knife. It was a fine art as he did it.

Henry Stender — photo taken about 1900

Edwin Carbery — my first cousin.

Another recollection is of the covered wagons we'd see as we went to and from school. They occasionally came through on roads in the vicinity of our homestead wandering over the country to find better opportunities. They camped beside the road wherever water was available. When the Nez Perce reservation was opened for settlement in the 1890's, several covered wagons went down the road past our farm. Some even camped on our place.

Bands of gypsies also traveled through the country in three or four wagons. They camped along the roads and, reputedly, lived off what they could steal. Nothing was ever stolen off our farm except a few bundles of hay.

But to my intense sorrow, our pet rooster who was our pride and joy, was carried off by a coyote one day.

SCHOOL NOT PLUSH IN EARLY DAY TEKOA

My first school stood at the top of the hill in the western edge of Tekoa. It was a tall, high-ceilinged, two store building and contained four rooms with two grades in each room. In the middle of each room was a cast-iron, wood burning stove. At regular intervals, the janitor would quietly slip in with an arm load of four-foot sticks of wood to stoke the stove. On cold days, those who sat near it roasted and those who sat by the windows shivered.

I do not remember that school was ever dismissed because of cold or stormy weather and at times the elements really howled around the school building, rattling all the windows.

There were no fire escapes and, if a fire had ever occurred, there would have been no way to get out even from the first floor as it was high above the basement and at the top of a flight of stairs.

When I first went to school I believe that drinking water was in pails with a dipper for each pail. Everybody used the same dippers. I do remember that later there was tap water at a wooden sink or drain where we could wash. Several tin cups sat on a shelf nearby for the use of whoever was thirsty.

Those who brought their lunches ate them in the basement where some benches were provided to sit on. Lunch pails were set on a deep shelf along one wall. Nearly everyone brought their lunch in a lard or tin pail of some sort. Later, I received a gift of a brown, kind of leatherette lunch box, square in shape and held together with a buckled strap.

Our school yard was divided into two parts. A high board fence ran from the middle of the back of the school to the end of the playground. The north side was the boys' side and the south belonged to the girls.

At the west end of the playground stood the outside "plumbing," four holers, I believe. Chloride of lime was thrown around liberally but was not too effective as a deodorant. These little houses were quite some distance from the school and a long wooden sidewalk led to each. On stormy days, we thought twice before raising one or two fingers to ask permission to go you-know-where. On sunny days, the trip out and back lasted as long as we felt we could stretch the walk.

On the girls' side of the school yard, the stovewood was piled and there was a lot of it. In the spring and fall when weather permitted, the girls constructed various playhouses out of the large slabs of fire wood. Groups of little girls industriously kept house at noon and recess and ate their lunches there. Rivalry was great as to which "family" had the nicest and roomiest houses.

The school house was entered by a rather long flight of steep stairs. Inside the double front door was a hall which led, right or left, to the two first floor rooms. Another flight led to the two rooms above.

Each time school was dismissed whether for noon, recess or end of the day, a boy with a drum stood on the landing and beat out time for marching and all the children marched in order from their class rooms. Those who did not keep step were hauled out of line and given marching lessons. On fair days, the lines formed outdoors, too, and we marched in to the drum beat. Later an organ was used for marching music.

When I was about a fourth or fifth grader, we played "run-sheep-run" or "hide and seek" all over the west hill. We ran 'til our tongues hung out trying not to be "it" or to lead one's "sheep" in safely. We also played "pom-pom-pull-away," and every spring, there was a rash of playing "statutes."

One or two of the teachers did open the windows once or twice a day, had us all stand up, breathe deeply and do calesthenics for a few minutes. This used to wake us up. Sometimes on Friday afternoons for an hour, we

I stayed at the Iwanbusch Boverman Pensionat from Oct. 1908 to April 1909. There was one girl from Holland. The two girls standing at the right are Mimi, from Monaco; and Germaine, from Belgium. I am the fourth from the left. Seated in front of me is Elsa, my best friend, who came from Finland. The other girls were from various provinces in Germany, and each spoke a slightly different dialect. I was several years older than most of the girls, who ranged from 16 to 18 or 19 years of age. Most were 16 and 17.

had ciphering or, perhaps, spelling matches. When I was in the eighth grade, there used to be debates.

So far as the primary teachers were concerned, they either lacked training or were indifferent for I did not learn to read, or write or do my numbers from them. A relative, who was living in our home, taught me how to read and write and the rudiments of arithmetic all in the matter of months. Until I learned to read, however, school was not a very happy place for me—I was more bewildered and hopeless than anything else. But with this new knowledge, school became a place of real challenge and excitement.

MOTHER'S SIDELINES SAVE FARMS IN 90'S PANIC

As we're finding out again, recessions and depressions seem to be a part of life in the United States but for the farmers of the Palouse the "panic" of the 1890's was a disaster.

It was only a coming of the railroad and the establishing of Tekoa as a division point of the Oregon-Washington Railroad and Navigation Company that saved the day for my parents.

Mother was overjoyed by the arrival of the railroad and the town so near the homestead but father was not so sure he liked being "crowded."

This steady payroll provided a base for the community's economy in the 1890s deep depression which was made even more frightening with the very wet year of 1894 when it was impossible to harvest the wheat crop.

Mother took advantage of this payroll and developed a sideline to augment the family income. She started selling good fresh eggs and butter. These were difficult to get in town in those days. As her fame for good things spread, she added garden vegetables, cheese, poultry, dressed and undressed, pork products and sauerkraut and all sorts of fruits from gooseberries and currants to prunes, apples and pears raised on our farm.

She had regular customers and delivered to them once a week until 1905 or 1906. Her sideline added enough income to save the farm through the panic years.

However, even when conditions improved, mother kept on with her "sideline" along with father's grain crops even though it meant long hours and back-breaking labors. With this double income, two more quarters

(320 acres) were bought, paid for and added to the original 160-acre homestead. One quarter section cost $3,300 in 1898 and sold for $75,000 in 1973.

Even though very young at the time, I recall the deep concern and worry of my parents about being able to meet the taxes and payments on the mortgage they had to put on the farm to keep going through the panic times. Finances got so low that father gave up smoking for a while and garbanza peas parched and ground were substituted for coffee.

These sacrifices made it possible, too, for father to accomplish his dream of his children having extensive educations.

By the time I had finished the tenth grade in the Tekoa school, in 1905, an eleventh grade was added and twelfth came soon. However, this school was not accredited and my father feared that I could not enter Washington Agricultural College at Pullman (now Washington State University) if I finished at Tekoa so I was shipped off to graduate from the Spokane High School.

Later I found out that the college was so anxious for students that practically no one was turned down. I could have presented my diploma from Tekoa and no questions asked.

In these 1970s, it would seem odd to say that it was an unusual idea to want children to go beyond the eighth grade and almost unheard of for a farm girl to be sent to college but that was the situation when I completed the eighth grade in 1903.

Tekoa's high school grades were accredited in 1909 when a class of six including my brother, Herman, graduated. My sister, Elfreda, graduated in 1916 with seven, the largest class in the school's history up to that time.

Interestingly, about that period the population of Tekoa was almost double what it is now yet the few children finishing high school reflected the community attitude toward higher education.

As visioned by our family, all us three Engelland children received degrees from Washington State College. I finished in 1912 with a bachelor's degree in English and German. Herman got an agricultural degree in 1915 and Elfreda graduated in pharmacy in 1920. Herman and I were the first native Tekoans to bring home college degrees and many of our parents contemporaries rather sneered at them for wasting money on sending their children to college.

I took up a career of high school teaching and followed it for 18 years. Herman farmed the family holdings until 1924 when he and his family moved to Tacoma and entered the grocery business. In 1920, women pharmacists were regarded with downright skepticism and it was almost impossible for them to secure good positions so Elfreda went on to nurses' training and became a registered nurse.

* * *

Thus the Engelland family had seen the town of Tekoa evolve from a few tents through a roaring railroad town to a pretty, quiet family community all in their life times. The bunch grass prairie homesteads had changed to great acreages of wheat and other cereals and the immigrant couples and their children have become a strong and integral part of America.

COLOPHON

The Bertha Engelland Williams PIONEER DAYS AT TEKOA *was printed in the workshop of Glen Adams, which is located in the sleepy country village of Fairfield, southern Spokane County in Washington state. Introduction was by Dale La Tendresse. The text was set in twelve point Baskerville type with two points of leading between the lines. Running heads were in eleven point Feinen and page numbers in twelve point Feinen. The typesetting was done by Kristy Frisbie, using a Compugraphic 48 and Editwriter 7300 computer photosetters. Camera-darkroom work was by Dale La Tendresse using a model 660C DS computer driven camera. The film was stripped by Pat Nigh, who also made the printing plates. The sheets were printed by Mike Fenich using a 28-inch model KORS Heidelberg press. The sheets were folded by Mike Fenich using a three-stage 22x28 inch Baum folding machine. Assembly and binding was by the Ye Galleon crew. Paper stock is Island Offset. This was a fun project. We had no special difficulty with the work.*